W9-BJT-836

DISCARD
THDRAWAL

‹VIETNAM›

MAJOR WORLD NATIONS

VIETNAM

Wendy M. Cole

CHELSEA HOUSE PUBLISHERS
Philadelphia

Chelsea House Publishers
Contributing Author: Margie Buckmaster

Copyright © 1999, 2001 by Chelsea House Publishers,
a subsidiary of Haights Cross Communications.
All rights reserved.
Printed and bound in Malaysia.

http://www.chelseahouse.com

5   7   9   8   6   4

◄CONTENTS►

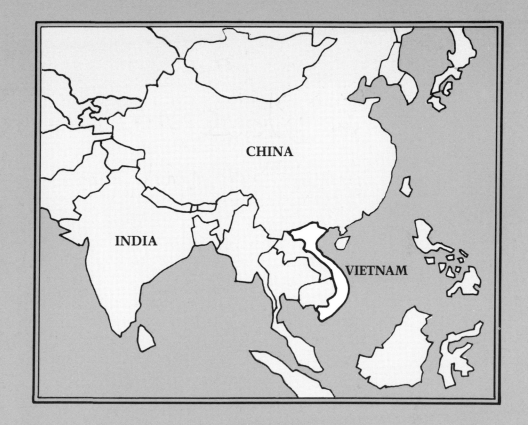

Land and People

Area	128,052 square miles (331,653 square kilometers)
Highest Point	Fan Si Pan, 10,312 feet (3,143 meters)
Population	74,000,000
Population Density	579 people per square mile
Population Distribution	Rural, 81 percent; urban, 19 percent
Capital	Hanoi (population 2,100,000)
Other Major Cities	Ho Chi Minh City (population 4,200,000) Haiphong (population 1,500,000)
National Language	Vietnamese
Religions	Buddhist, 55 percent; Taoist, Confucian, Roman Catholic, Muslim, Hoa Hao, and Cao Dai are other main denominations. Most Vietnamese practice more than one religion
Ethnic Groups	Vietnamese, 85 percent; the remainder of the population is divided between Chinese, Tai, Khmer, Muong, Thai, Nung, Meo, Man, Jarai, and Cham
Literacy Rate	94 percent
Average Life Expectancy	67 years
Infant Mortality Rate	39 deaths per 1,000 births

Economy

Mineral Resources	Phosphates, coal, iron, manganese
Employment	Agriculture, forestry, and fishing, 65 percent of population; industry and commerce, 35 percent
Major Cash Crops	Rice, sugar, cassava, sweet potato, rubber
Industries	Food processing, textiles, cement, fertilizer
Currency	Dong, divided into 10 hao

Government

Form of Government	Socialist republic
Government Bodies	The Communist Party's governing council, the Politburo, sets national policy and exercises control over all governmental bodies. Legislative power is held by the National Assembly, whose representatives are elected by the people every 5 years.
Regional Administrative Organizations	The country's 50 provinces and 3 municipalities are governed by administrative bodies known as People's Councils
Head of State	President
Other Chief Officials	Prime minister, deputy prime ministers
Eligibility to Vote	All citizens 18 years or older

◄HISTORY AT A GLANCE►

3000 to 1000 B.C.	Groups of nomadic tribes from southern China migrate into the Red River Delta region and merge with Indonesian peoples already living there.
about 250 B.C.	Legend says that the kingdom of Au Lac rules Vietnam.
207 B.C.	A Chinese general establishes the independent kingdom of Nam-Viet, which consists of northern Vietnam and parts of southern China.
111 B.C.	China's Han dynasty conquers Nam-Viet, renames it Giao Chi, and makes it the southernmost province of the Chinese Empire.
A.D. 679	Chinese change the name of the country to Annam.
939	The Vietnamese win independence from China and set up an independent state under the rule of the Ngo dynasty.
1010 to 1225	The Ly family rules Vietnam.
about 1200	Chu-nom, a transcription of Vietnamese words in simplified Chinese characters, comes into use.
1225 to 1400	Vietnam ruled by the Tran dynasty, during whose reign two invasions by China's Mongol rulers are turned back.
1427	Le Loi expels Chinese armies from Vietnam, ending a 20-year-period of foreign occupation. Le Loi founds the Le dynasty, which conquers

Champa and extends Vietnam's territory far to the south.

1527 to 1593   Vietnam ruled by the Mac family.

1535   Portuguese traders visit Vietnam.

about 1600   French traders and missionaries begin to establish posts in Vietnam.

1620 to 1672   Nguyen and Trinh families battle for control of Vietnam, finally agreeing to divide the country into northern and southern kingdoms.

1772 to 1786   Tay Son peasant rebels defeat Nguyen and Trinh armies and unite Vietnam under their rule.

about 1800   Nguyen Du composes Vietnam's national poem, *Kim Van Kieu.*

1802   Nguyen Anh defeats Tay Son rulers and unites country under rule of the Nguyen dynasty.

about 1820   Nguyen rulers begin persecution of Catholic missionaries and their converts.

1847   The French launch first major attack against the Vietnamese, firing on the port of Da Nang.

1858 to 1883   The French gain control of Vietnam and divide the country into three separate colonial provinces.

about 1900   Phan Boi Chau and other nationalist leaders begin to form a strong resistance movement against French colonial rulers.

1910 to 1939   Two radical Vietnamese religious sects, Cao Dai and Hoa Hao, are founded.

1940 to 1945   Japan takes control of Vietnam from France during World War II. Millions of Vietnamese die during wartime famine.

1941   Ho Chi Minh forms the Vietminh, an alliance of nationalist groups led by the Communist party.

1975   South Vietnam surrenders to North Vietnam on April 30. The united nation is organized under the name of the Socialist Republic of Vietnam. The boat-people exodus begins.

1978   Vietnam invades and occupies Cambodia.

1979   Vietnam fights a border war with China.

1986   Conservative leaders of Vietnam's ruling Politburo resign, opening the way for moderate social and economic reforms.

1987   Vietnam announces reforms aimed at reducing central control of the economy.

1994   The United States ends a 19-year embargo on trade with Vietnam.

1995   The United States extends full diplomatic recognition to Vietnam.

1997   A U.S. ambassador is stationed in Vietnam for the first time in more than 20 years.

2000   President Bill Clinton visits Vietnam, the first U.S. president to visit the country since the end of the Vietnam War.

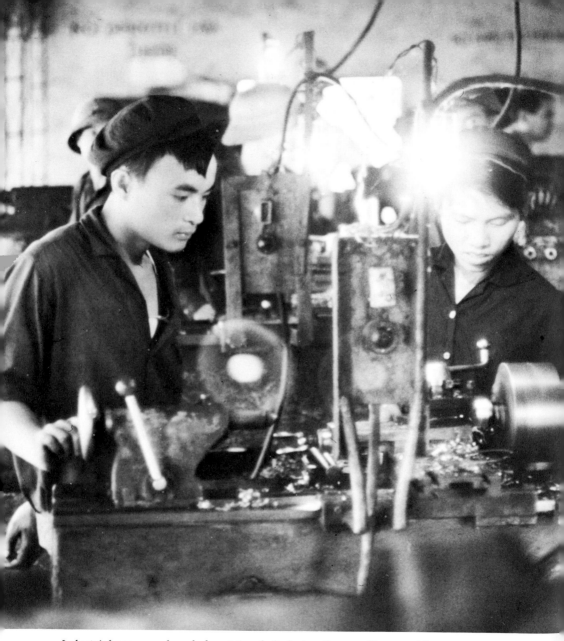

Industrial progress slowed almost to a halt during the war. These cart factory workers are employed as part of Vietnam's new industrialization effort.

1975 South Vietnam surrenders to North Vietnam on April 30. The united nation is organized under the name of the Socialist Republic of Vietnam. The boat-people exodus begins.

1978 Vietnam invades and occupies Cambodia.

1979 Vietnam fights a border war with China.

1986 Conservative leaders of Vietnam's ruling Politburo resign, opening the way for moderate social and economic reforms.

1987 Vietnam announces reforms aimed at reducing central control of the economy.

1994 The United States ends a 19-year embargo on trade with Vietnam.

1995 The United States extends full diplomatic recognition to Vietnam.

1997 A U.S. ambassador is stationed in Vietnam for the first time in more than 20 years.

One of Hanoi's most beloved shrines, the One-Pillar Pagoda, was built in 1049. It stands in a lily pond and is reached by a stone staircase.

Vietnam and
the World

Stretching more than 1,000 miles (1,600 kilometers) from high, misty mountains in the north to the flat delta of the Mekong River in the south, Vietnam is a land of arresting scenic beauty. Poised like an S-shaped dragon on the eastern side of Southeast Asia (one of Vietnam's traditional national symbols, the dragon is the token of nobility and power) Vietnam occupies a strategic position near some of the world's most powerful countries. Once a land that attracted little attention outside of Asia, Vietnam has in recent times found itself at the center of international power struggles.

From their beginnings as a farming tribe in northern Vietnam, the fiercely independent Vietnamese have fought with other peoples to win control of their country. For long periods during their history, the Vietnamese have been ruled by foreign powers. In the last century, the country was split into three sections and absorbed into the French colonial domain of Indochina. Resistance to French domination fueled the growth of many independence groups, including the Vietnamese Communist party. At the end of World War II, the communist Vietminh alliance gained control of northern Vietnam and eventually defeated French attempts to restore their colonial power. The end of French rule was followed by an 18-year struggle between the North Vietnamese government and the anticommunist and United States-backed regime that was elected to govern South Vietnam.

In 1975, the North Vietnamese took control of the entire country and established the Socialist Republic of Vietnam. The Vietnamese paid a tragically high price for the unification of their country. During the civil war between the North and the South—a struggle that is known in the United States as the Vietnam War—the countryside was pounded by American bombs and millions of Vietnamese were killed in the fighting. The war's devastating effect on Vietnam's agriculture and industry and on the political stability of Southeast Asia continues to be felt.

After the war, Vietnamese leaders struggled to reunite the northern and southern halves of the country. Schooled more in the arts of war than in the business of managing a national economy, government officials at first had limited success in their efforts to revive the country's war-torn farms, factories, and transportation system. The rebuilding process was also hampered by racial conflicts between the country's minority groups and the native ethnic group, the Vietnamese. During the 1970s and 1980s, hundreds of thousands of members of the ethnic minorities and opponents of the communist government fled Vietnam. The country sorely felt the loss of a sizable proportion of its productive workforce.

Nevertheless, Vietnam began to assert its identity as a power in Asia. Though it remained dependent upon the now-disbanded Soviet Union for much military and economic assistance, Vietnam followed an independent course in foreign affairs. For years it maintained an openly hostile relationship with China and, ignoring the protests of other Southeast Asian nations and the United States, it invaded Cambodia in 1979 and occupied that country for the next ten years.

By the late 1980s, saddled with a deteriorating economy and a dire need to modernize its industries, Vietnam began to relax its central control of the economy and allow room for free enterprise. The collapse of the Soviet Union meant that Vietnam had to turn elsewhere for much of its assistance, and in the 1990s it began to attract substantial foreign investment. At last the economy began to expand rapidly.

Meanwhile, relations with the United States were finally normalized. In 1994, in response to Vietnam's cooperation in the search for missing American soldiers, the United States ended its long economic embargo. In July 1995 a resumption of full diplomatic relations between the two countries was announced, and less than two years later, a new U.S. ambassador took up residence in Vietnam. Similarly, Vietnam began a rapprochement with China.

Despite these hopeful signs, many economic and political challenges remain. How the Vietnamese respond to these challenges will determine whether the country can play a prominent role in guiding the future development of Southeast Asia.

Water—whether the ocean, rivers and lakes, or simply that which floods the rice paddies—is part of everyday life for most people. These are fishing boats on the southern coast.

Land of
Two Rice Baskets

Because of the peculiar, curving shape that Vietnam forms as it hugs the eastern coast of Southeast Asia, the country is sometimes described by the Vietnamese as being two rice baskets hanging from opposite ends of a farmer's pole. In the north, the area around the intensively cultivated Red River Delta forms one "basket." Extending southward from the delta flatlands, a narrow corridor of small fertile plains and rocky coastal promontories creates "the carrying pole." In the far south, the rich soil of the Mekong River Delta forms the other "basket."

Along with Myanmar, Thailand, Laos, and Cambodia, Vietnam is located on the Indochinese Peninsula. Jutting out from the southern end of China, this peninsula is home to almost half of the nations of Southeast Asia (which also include Malaysia, Singapore, Indonesia, New Guinea, Brunei, and the Philippines). The geography of the Indochinese Peninsula features numerous mountain ranges, river valleys, and forested plains.

To the east of Vietnam lie the South China Sea and the Gulf of Tonkin, which are part of the Pacific Ocean. Vietnam is separated from its western neighbors, Laos and Cambodia, by the Annamite Mountains. This mountain range extends from the Chinese border in the north to the extensive plateau of Vietnam's central highlands. Around the country's southern border, the land flattens out in the delta region where the Mekong River flows out of Cambodia and into Vietnam.

Vietnam has a total land area of 128,052 square miles (331,653 square kilometers), roughly the same size as New Mexico and about three-quarters the size of California. The country reaches a maximum width of about 350 miles (560 kilometers) in the north, and it narrows to about 40 miles (64 kilometers) in its central areas. From its northern border to its southern tip, Vietnam is about 1,000 miles (1,600 kilometers) long, and it has a coastline of more than 1,400 miles (2,250 kilometers). Only about 20 percent of the land is composed of the flat river areas that the Vietnamese can use for farming. The remainder consists of heavily forested and mountainous regions. Most Vietnamese live along the coast or in the delta areas.

Geographical Regions

Vietnam has five major land regions, ranging from the highlands in the north to the Mekong Delta in the south. The Annamite Mountains, the Red River Delta, and the Mekong Delta are the three features that dominate Vietnam's geography.

The northern highlands are part of a mountainous region in northwestern Vietnam that extends into China and Laos. Forests or jungles cover most of the mountains in this sparsely populated region. The highest peak in Vietnam, Fan Si Pan, rises to a height of 10,312 feet (3,143 meters) a few miles distant from where the Red River slices through the northern highlands. The region contains the bulk of the country's coal, iron, and other mineral resources.

The second region, the Red River Delta, extends from the northern highlands to the Gulf of Tonkin. The delta is formed by the division of the Red River into many widely separated branches as it flows into the gulf. Most of the delta lies 10 feet (3 meters) or less

Wearing the traditional straw hat of the countryside, a woman herds ducklings in the Mekong River Delta region.

above sea level, and during the summer flood season, the river often overflows the dikes that the Vietnamese have constructed along the river banks. The fertile Red River Delta is densely populated and is northern Vietnam's main farming area. The region includes two of Vietnam's largest cities, Hanoi and Haiphong.

The central highlands are a narrow strip of mountainous territory running down the spine of Vietnam's western border. Part of the huge Annamite Mountain range, the area reaches to within a few miles of Ho Chi Minh City (formerly known as Saigon) at its southern extent. Forests cover most of the mountains in this thinly populated region, but its plateaus are home to some of Vietnam's nomadic tribes.

The coastal lowlands occupy the eastern strip of central Vietnam between the Red River and Mekong deltas. The lowlands are crossed by many small rivers and streams that are fed by the runoff from storms in the central highlands. Rice is grown throughout most of this heavily populated region, but many people living in the coastal

The Customs House dominates this view of Ho Chi Minh City (formerly the South Vietnamese capital city of Saigon).

villages earn their living through fishing. The largest cities in the region are Hue and Da Nang.

The fifth region, the Mekong Delta, covers all of Vietnam south of the central highlands and the coastal lowlands. The Mekong River—which runs for 2,600 miles (4,200 kilometers) from southern China to its mouth on the South China Sea—has gradually formed this region with its deposits of silt. Like the Red River Delta, the Mekong Delta lies 10 feet (3 meters) or less above sea level, and parts of it are often flooded during the late summer and early fall. More than half the people of southern Vietnam live on the delta, and it is the country's most productive agricultural area. The chief city in the region is Ho Chi Minh City, which is located on the Saigon River.

Climate

Vietnam has a tropical climate, and its populated lowland areas have relatively small ranges in temperature from winter to summer. Most of the country has two seasons—a wet, hot summer and a drier, cooler winter. However, some of the highland areas have four distinct seasons. From May to October, the land is swept by the seasonal wind known as the summer monsoon, which brings heavy rains from the southwest. The winter monsoon brings drier air from the Asian mainland. The amount of rainfall that the monsoons bring from year to year varies greatly. Famines have frequently occurred in Vietnam when a year of drought has been followed by a year of heavy floods.

The national economy is based on agriculture. Most work is done by hand and with handmade tools like this watering system.

Northern Vietnam's heavily populated areas have moderate temperatures and light rainfall from November to April. The average January temperature in Hanoi is about 63° Fahrenheit (17° Centigrade). From May to October, the Red River Delta has high temperatures and heavy rainfall. Hanoi's average temperature during June is 85° F (29° C). The capital's annual rainfall averages about 72 inches (1,800 millimeters).

In southern Vietnam, the humidity stays high all year, but the area receives almost all of its rain between April and November. The temperature in Ho Chi Minh City ranges from about 79° F (26° C) in December to 85° F (29° C) in April. The city's annual rainfall is about 80 inches (2,000 mm).

Vietnam's central and northern highlands are cooler and less humid than the coastal regions. The central lowlands receive the most rain of any area in the country, and Hue sometimes records more than 120 inches (3,000 mm) of precipitation in years when the summer monsoon brings especially heavy storms from the South China Sea.

Plants and Animals

More than three-quarters of Vietnam is covered by forests. Deciduous hardwoods, evergreens, and bamboos are common in the northern forests, which produce commercially valuable woods such as mahogany, teak, chestnut, rosewood, and ebony. Tropical pines and palms blanket the southern highlands. In the delta marshlands, mangrove trees and tall grasses are abundant.

Vietnam's rain forests include a wide variety of flowers, bushes, and vines. Some of the plants are of great beauty, including some spectacular orchids. The jungles also have some extremely dangerous plants, such as a shrub that produces painful skin blisters when it is touched. In the past, Vietnamese soldiers have prepared deadly arrows by dipping them in the poisonous sap of giant sack trees.

The Vietnamese have introduced many domesticated plants to their country's natural habitat. Some of the commonly grown agricultural plants of the lowland areas include rice, tea, coffee, cacao, tobacco, sugarcane, corn, cassavas, and sweet potatoes. Rubber trees are often raised in upland areas.

Vietnam has a tremendous number of animal species, and the country was considered a hunter's paradise in the French colonial era. Tigers, panthers, bears, jackals, deer, wild oxen, elephants, boars, goats, and wild dogs roam the highland areas. Gibbons and many other kinds of monkeys live in the forests, and a large number of bird species, including peacocks, partridges, and ducks, can be found throughout the country. Fishermen hunt sharks, eels, and sea turtles off the coast, and carp and catfish are caught in the rivers. Among the dangerous reptiles that people must avoid are cobras, pythons, and crocodiles.

Vietnam's history includes many eras of warfare, rebellion, and invasion—and additional suffering for those, like this family, who have been forced to flee their homes as refugees.

A Land
of Struggle

The ancestral homeland of the Vietnamese is the Red River Delta in northern Vietnam. Many legends have arisen to explain the origin and ancient history of the Vietnamese, but only a few facts can be determined from early records. Between 5,000 and 3,000 years ago, a tribe migrated from southern China to the Red River valley. After seizing control of the region from one of the Indonesian peoples who had previously settled along the eastern coast of Southeast Asia, the invaders merged with the conquered group to form the original Vietnamese people.

Using agricultural techniques that had been practiced in China for centuries, the Vietnamese drained parts of the Red River Delta's marshlands and turned the fields into irrigated rice paddies. The Vietnamese fought a constant battle with floods, storms, and droughts to win a living from their land. Because close cooperation between rice farmers was necessary for maintaining the walls of the network of dikes that protected the square paddies, the Vietnamese soon developed a tightly knit society ruled by a strong central government. They remained in the lowland regions and generally avoided the mountainous inland regions, which they believed to be inhabited by evil spirits.

Many rulers faced outside enemies. Emperor Tu Duc fought the French in the 1800s.

As their population grew, the Vietnamese gradually expanded their territory. Vietnamese legends tell of a number of ancient kingdoms. During the 3d century B.C., the kingdom of Au Lac is supposed to have ruled present-day northern Vietnam. The kingdoms were organized in a feudal system, with a small class of nobles and their attendants ruling over a much larger body of small landowners and peasants. Life and work were centered around the growing and harvesting of rice, and one of the main duties of the royal officials was to make sure that surplus grain was set aside and stored for the years when rains were light and famines occurred.

The early Vietnamese kingdoms were closely tied to the Chinese empire's southern provinces. In 207 B.C., a Chinese general named Trieu Da conquered the Au Lac kingdom and established the independent kingdom of Nam-Viet, which included the northern half of present-day Vietnam and most of southeastern China. This Chinese-Vietnamese kingdom lasted for nearly a century. In 111 B.C., the rulers of China's powerful Han dynasty conquered Nam-Viet, renamed it Giao Chi, and made it the southernmost province of the Chinese Empire.

The Vietnamese were ruled by China for more than 1,000 years, and their culture was strongly influenced by Chinese arts, religions, politics, and agricultural methods. But despite China's attempts to absorb the people of Giao Chi into its vast empire, the Vietnamese remained a fiercely independent people.

In the 1st century A.D., the Trung sisters, two Vietnamese noblewomen, led a revolt against repressive imperial rulers and established a short-lived Vietnamese kingdom. Later, the Vietnamese made further attempts to win their independence. In 248, Vietnamese rebels led by the noblewoman Trieu Au were defeated by the imperial armies. But three centuries later, a general named Ly Bon defeated the Chinese and crowned himself emperor. The Chinese quickly regained control of the region. In 679, they changed the name of the province from Giao Chi to Annam.

Early in the 10th century, China's imperial authority was weakened by internal rebellions. In 939, the Vietnamese were finally able to wrest their independence from the Chinese emperors. To placate their former overlords, the first rulers of Vietnam, the Ngo dynasty, officially acknowledged China's power by paying a regular tribute in the form of precious gifts, including ivory and gold.

Although the Vietnamese continued to resent China's dominance, Vietnam's scholars were heavily influenced by Chinese culture. Chinese characters were used for the written language, and many elements of the Chinese educational system and government were adopted by Vietnam's rulers. Vietnamese temples and the buildings of the royal court were modeled on Chinese designs that featured structures with high stone walls, cylindrical columns, and sloping, tiled roofs. However, despite the powerful influence of the Chinese, the strong-willed Vietnamese preserved a separate national identity.

Two other imports from China that had a great impact on Vietnamese culture were Buddhism and Confucianism. A religion of Indian origin, Buddhism teaches that one can escape from life's suffering by striving for a state of high moral and spiritual purity.

The Confucianist religious philosophy, which set forth a code of moral conduct for righteous rulers and their dutiful subjects, was especially popular with the Vietnamese nobles.

Between 939 and 1427, there was a central kingship in Vietnam, but wealthy, aristocratic families battled for power. The Ngo dynasty was replaced by other ruling families, and the Ly and Tran dynasties both had 200-year reigns over Vietnam. Successful dynasties had a three-fold task: to maintain their authority against internal competitors, to protect the country against Chinese invasion, and to provide land for Vietnam's expanding population. The Tran enlarged the system of dikes on the Red River and brought extensive areas of new land into cultivation.

Despite their closeness to the sea and their reputation for being the best sailors in East Asia, the Vietnamese remained tied to their land and rice growing and gave only secondary importance to maritime trade. However, the country was heavily dependent on the fishermen who worked the coastal waters and provided a vital food staple for Vietnam's rice-based diet. Fearing the sudden storms that

In 1284 and 1287, the Mongol ruler Kublai Khan was defeated in his attempts to reestablish Chinese rule over Vietnam.

often swept in over the South China Sea, the fishermen painted the eyes or heads of dragons on their boats to frighten the evil water spirits who were believed to stir up the sea.

The Chinese never gave up their hopes of reconquering Vietnam. In 1284 and 1287, the Kublai Khan, the Mongol ruler of China, sent huge armies to conquer Vietnam. Both times, the Mongol armies were defeated. Later, however, Vietnam suffered a series of defeats at the hands of neighboring kingdoms to the south and west and, in 1407, the Chinese regained control of the country. A resistance movement founded by a landowner named Le Loi fought back against the invaders and drove them out of the capital, Hanoi. In 1427, the victorious Le Loi proclaimed himself emperor of Vietnam, thus establishing the Le dynasty.

An Expanding Kingdom

From the time of their arrival in the Red River region, the Vietnamese had been partially shielded from other kingdoms on the Indochinese peninsula by the western mountain ranges. Under the Le dynasty, Vietnam began to push southward. In the past, the Vietnamese had fought frequent wars with the Chams, whose kingdom of Champa included most of what is now the central part of Vietnam. Like the Khmers, who occupied the southern part of the Indochinese peninsula, the Chams practiced the Hindu religion and were heavily influenced by the Indian civilization. A seafaring people, the Chams had sailed north on several occasions and defeated Vietnamese armies, once burning Hanoi.

During the 1400s, the Vietnamese defeated the Chams and established Vietnamese settlements and military colonies throughout Champa. The conquest of the southern territories opened up new landholdings for the Vietnamese peasantry, and the kingdom's wealth and military power were greatly increased. The Le rulers introduced humane legal codes that gave property ownership rights to women, who in Vietnamese society had a much lower social position than men. The ruling dynasty also carried out land reforms that aided the peasants.

By this time, Confucianism had almost completely replaced Buddhism as the dominant religion in Vietnam. Confucianist teachings emphasized the importance of knowledge and learning, and Vietnamese provinces were administered by royal officials known as mandarins, who were well-schooled in Confucianist teachings. Young men studied for examinations in Confucianist philosophy that determined whether they were fit to become mandarins.

Although most new developments in the arts occurred at the royal court and in the larger cities, the village remained the backbone of Vietnamese society. Each village elected its own officials, who were responsible for maintaining order, trying court cases, and making sure that taxes were collected. In the delta regions, villagers spent much of the year repairing dikes, digging canals to divert floodwaters, and working on other public projects. Villages were located beside the dike embankments and were connected to each other by paths that ran along the tops of the walls. Village families were aligned in large clans, whose members met to practice sacred rituals such as the honoring of the clan's ancestors.

Vietnam had only short periods of domestic peace during the reign of the Le dynasty, and the country was racked by constant fighting between competing aristocratic families. Although the Le continued to hold the title of emperor until near the end of the 18th century, they had lost almost all control of the government by 1500.

In the mid-1500s, Vietnam was divided between two powerful families, the Mac and the Trinh. After more than 60 years of warfare, the Trinh defeated their rivals and reunited their divided land. But in the early 1600s, Vietnam was split apart once more by the struggle between the Trinh, who ruled from Hanoi in the north, and the Nguyen family, who controlled the southern part of the kingdom.

Both families claimed to support the Le emperors, and the Trinh launched many campaigns against the South. However, the Nguyen built two strong walls across the northern border of their land and repulsed every Trinh attack. The Nguyen were given military assistance by the Dutch, who in return were granted the right to establish trading centers in the South.

In 1672, the Trinh and the Nguyen families signed a truce and divided Vietnam near the present-day city of Qang Tri. During the following century of peace, the Nguyen attacked the Khmer kingdom of Cambodia and conquered the rest of the eastern coast of the Indochinese peninsula, including the Mekong Delta. By the mid-18th century, the Vietnamese occupied most of the territory that comprise present-day Vietnam.

Beginning in the 16th century, Europeans began to play an increasingly important role in East Asian affairs. In 1535, the Portuguese established a trading post in Vietnam. They were followed by the Dutch, British, and French, who battled with each other for control of the rich Asian trade in silk, tea, ivory, and spices. The Europeans were unable to dominate Vietnam as they did other parts of Southeast Asia, because both the northern and southern areas of Vietnam had strong governments and fought off the Europeans' attempts to build colonial bases in Indochina.

The Vietnamese nations remained feudal societies ruled by aristocratic landowners who severely exploited the peasantry. Famines, marauding bandits, and greedy tax collectors added to the troubles of the peasants, who grew increasingly restless about their wretched living conditions. Calling out for sweeping social reforms that would benefit the poor, the peasants engaged in widespread rebellions that undermined the authority of the Nguyen and Trinh. Having served in the armies that had defended Vietnam against foreign invaders, the peasants felt a strong sense of national pride and were committed to saving the country from corrupt administrators.

In 1772, three brothers (who were named for their home, the central Vietnamese village of Tay Son) organized a peasant rebellion that quickly grew into a powerful national movement. The rebels overthrew the Nguyen in 1777 and then marched north and defeated the Trinh after a nine-year struggle. The youngest Tay Son brother declared himself emperor.

The Tay Son ruled over a united Vietnam for only a short period. Nguyen Anh, a member of the defeated Nguyen family, won control of the South with the help of French mercenaries. Popular support for the Tay Son died when the brothers failed to take steps to improve social conditions for the common people. By 1802, Nguyen Anh had defeated the Tay Son and crowned himself emperor of Vietnam under the name Gia Long.

French Control

Under Gia Long and succeeding emperors of the Nguyen dynasty, Vietnam enjoyed a period of national unity. Much of the country's network of canals and dikes had fallen into disrepair during the previous years of tumult, and Gia Long established a huge national public works program to restore crumbling structures and build new bridges and castles. To help bind the nation together, the Nguyen constructed a wide road from Hanoi to Saigon. They also formed a strong war fleet to protect Vietnam's coastline.

The Nguyen left most of the responsibilities of administering Vietnam's provinces to local governors and thus had little contact with the common people. Gradually, some of the provincial lords began to challenge the authority of the ruling dynasty. The Nguyen emperors crushed most of the revolts, but their increasing isolation from their subjects left the country vulnerable to foreign intrusions.

The assault on Vietnam's independence was not long in coming. By the early 1800s, the French had decided to establish a strong foothold in Indochina. French merchants and Catholic missionaries, who had begun setting up trading posts and churches in Vietnam in the 1600s, helped spread French influence in the country. Tens of thousands of Vietnam's peasants were converted to Christianity by Catholic priests, who encouraged the French government to set up a colonial state in Vietnam.

The Nguyen emperors became increasingly suspicious about the intentions of the Catholic missionaries. After large numbers of Vietnamese Christians were implicated in plots to overthrow the government, the emperors began a large-scale persecution of the missionaries. In the 1830s, several missionaries were executed and many more expelled from the country. Vietnam's distrust of France and other Western nations was further increased in the 1840s, after the British attacked Chinese ports and forced China to make humiliating trade concessions.

The Vietnamese government rejected French attempts to negotiate commercial treaties and continued to persecute Catholic missionaries. In 1847, the French navy retaliated by firing upon the port of Da Nang, killing hundreds of Vietnamese. The French followed up their initial attack by sending a large expeditionary force to southern Vietnam in 1858.

The French invasion coincided with peasant revolts in northern Vietnam. Tu Duc, the reigning emperor, suppressed the rebellions, but his troops were unable to stop the French. By 1867, the emperor had been forced to allow French control over the southernmost quarter of Vietnam, which the French called Cochin China. During this period, the French also seized control of Cambodia.

France continued its battle for an empire in Southeast Asia. Vietnamese independence ended in 1883, when a French army forced the imperial court to grant the French the right to govern the rest of the country. Although the Vietnamese emperor was allowed to hold on to his throne, his role became mainly ceremonial. The French divided Vietnam into three colonial states: Cochin China (southern Vietnam), Annam (central Vietnam), and Tonkin (northern Vietnam). France governed these areas as separate parts of French Indochina, which also included Cambodia and Laos.

During the following six decades, the French built up a strong colonial system in Indochina. The French colonial administration claimed that it was providing the Vietnamese with an efficient government, improved medical, educational, and transportation systems, and a more prosperous economy. In reality, the French often treated the Vietnamese brutally and were mainly interested in exploiting Indochina's agriculture and minerals. To help French settlers build large plantations, the colonial governors seized land from the peasants and forced them to become landless laborers. The French constructed dams, canals, and railroads throughout the country, but these public works programs were often extremely wasteful and were a huge burden on the overtaxed Vietnamese people.

French rule left a deep mark on the Vietnamese, introducing them to Western learning and customs and expanding their global outlook. Some Vietnamese scholars attended universities in France

In the 1920s, Ho Chi Minh began to establish himself as the leader of Vietnam's Communist party.

and helped to further scientific research in their own country. However, the broadening of Vietnam's cultural base was acquired at the expense of traditional Vietnamese learning, which was scorned by the French and ignored in public schools.

Vietnamese resentment of French rule spurred the growth of a vigorous liberation movement in the early 20th century. The nationalist leader Phan Boi Chau was especially active in organizing protests against the colonial administration. The French retaliated with beatings, arrests, and sometimes even executions of Vietnamese patriots. The liberation movement was checked for the moment, but the Vietnamese desire for independence could not be stifled forever.

The Struggle for Independence

In 1939, World War II broke out in Europe. Early in the war, Germany invaded France and forced it to surrender. The conflict became a struggle between the Axis powers (Germany, Italy, and Japan) and the Allies (Britain, the United States, and the Soviet Union). While the Germans fought to dominate Europe, their ally Japan was trying to create an empire in eastern Asia. After invading China in the early 1930s, Japan pushed southward. By the early 1940s, the Japanese troops occupied all of Southeast Asia.

Japan allowed French colonial officials to govern Indochina but forced them to follow the orders of the Japanese occupation forces. As France's hold over Indochina began to slip, Vietnamese nationalist groups gained control over areas of the Vietnamese countryside. The Indochinese Communist party, a group that supported radical social reforms such as seizing land from wealthy landlords and giving it to peasants, emerged as the most powerful of the resistance groups. In 1941, the Communists' leader, Ho Chi Minh, organized a coalition of liberation groups known as the Vietminh. During World War II, the Vietminh gave the Allies information about Japanese troop movements.

Although little fighting occurred in Vietnam during World War II, the Vietnamese suffered terribly from famine. As many as 2 million people may have starved to death in northern Vietnam during the last year of the war. By early 1945, the tide of the war had turned against Japan. After the Allies freed France from German control, the Japanese decided that French colonial administrators in Indochina could no longer be trusted. In March 1945, the Japanese arrested all French officials in Vietnam and set up a new government headed by the Vietnamese emperor Bao Dai. The Japanese declared that Vietnam was an independent nation, but it was still supervised by Japan's armies.

In August 1945, Japan surrendered to the Allies and gave up control over Southeast Asia. Backed by popular support, the Vietminh quickly assumed power and forced Bao Dai to step down as ruler. On September 2, 1945, Ho Chi Minh, the leader of the new government, announced the formation of a united Vietnam under the name of the Democratic Republic of Vietnam (DRV). The seat of government was Hanoi.

The Vietnamese still had a long battle ahead for their independence. Refusing to give up control over their former Indochinese colony, the French struck back. In late 1945, their troops regained control of Cochin China, the southern part of Vietnam. Hoping to avoid a war with the French, Ho Chi Minh agreed to allow French troops to establish bases in northern Vietnam in return for French recognition of the DRV. But each side accused the other of violating treaty obligations, and in December 1946, the French-Indochina War broke out between the Vietminh and the French.

For more than 7 years, French colonial troops battled Vietminh guerrilla fighters. The heavily armed French troops controlled all the major cities, but they were unable to crush the mobile, elusive Vietminh. Based in the rural areas of northern Vietnam, the Vietminh maintained good relations with the peasants and enlisted them

French troops, weary of trying to subdue the communist Vietminh, withdrew from Vietnam in 1954 after their defeat at Dien Bien Phu.

into their nationalist revolution. In 1949, the French set up a Vietnamese government headed by Emperor Bao Dai to oppose the Vietminh, but it attracted little support from the people. The Vietminh, on the other hand, continued to increase their strength with military assistance from the Soviet Union and the newly established communist Chinese republic.

In the early 1950s, the French position in Vietnam began to crumble. On May 7, 1954, a French army stationed at the fortress of Dien Bien Phu in northern Vietnam was forced to surrender to the Vietminh. Two months later, representatives of the Vietminh, the Bao Dai government, France, Cambodia, Laos, China, the Soviet Union, the United States, and other nations met in Geneva, Switzerland, to negotiate an end to the French-Indochina War and French rule in Southeast Asia.

The agreement signed at the Geneva Conference stated that Vietnam would temporarily be divided into two parts until elections

could be held to form a unified government. A communist government headed by Ho Chi Minh would rule North Vietnam, and Emperor Bao Dai's government would rule South Vietnam. The border
between the two states was close to the line that had divided the
Trinh and Nguyen kingdoms in the 17th and 18th centuries. Hanoi
was the capital of the North, and Saigon was the capital of the South.

A Nation Divided

The two Vietnamese governments quickly developed a bitter enmity
toward each other, and any chance for forming a united country
disappeared. In the North, the Communists eliminated all political
opponents and set about building a highly structured socialist nation
with a state-controlled economy. In the South, political power was
divided among many groups, including some that supported a communist government for all of Vietnam. However, the deeply anticommunist prime minister of South Vietnam, Ngo Dinh Diem,
rallied the forces in the South that opposed cooperating with the
Hanoi regime. His faction soon emerged as the strongest group in
Saigon.

In 1955, Diem deposed Bao Dai, seized control of the South
Vietnamese government, and had himself appointed president. Diem
canceled plans for an election to choose a united national government, stating that the Hanoi regime would never allow free elections
in the North. Meanwhile, Diem suppressed all political opposition in
the South and unleashed the army against the Communist groups,
which had bases in the rural areas. With the aid of the North Vietnamese, the southern Communist groups formed a resistance movement known as the National Liberation Front (NLF) and drove
Diem's troops from the countryside.

Diem's corrupt, authoritarian rule was strongly criticized by the
South Vietnamese, and he was able to remain in power only because
he received massive military and economic assistance from the

United States. The American government was determined to stop the spread of communism throughout Southeast Asia and feared that South Vietnam would fall to the NLF if Diem were forced out of office.

By 1963, the popular feelings against Diem's repressive policies had grown too strong, and the United States withdrew its support for the president. A group of military officers overthrew and killed Diem. The new government was fully committed to the war against the communist rebels, whom it called the Viet Cong, and the Americans promised the Saigon government greater military support.

The fighting in South Vietnam developed into a major war. In August 1964, American and North Vietnamese ships had two hostile engagements in the Gulf of Tonkin. The United States declared that it had been attacked, launched immediate bombing strikes against North Vietnam, and began sending thousands of troops to South Vietnam to back up the Saigon government. With the assistance of the United States, Australia, New Zealand, South Korea, and other allies, the South Vietnamese government renewed its attempt to expel the NLF from its strongholds in the countryside.

The U.S. and South Vietnamese armies tried to overwhelm the NLF guerrillas and their North Vietnamese allies with a punishing display of firepower. American bombers raided Hanoi and other cities in the North and destroyed dams, bridges, and railroads. South Vietnamese forests were sprayed with herbicides such as Agent Orange to strip them of their foliage so that American troops could locate guerrilla outposts. The NLF suffered heavy casualties, but its fighting spirit remained high. The guerrillas kept themselves supplied with captured weapons and with arms from North Vietnam that were brought down the "Ho Chi Minh trail," a network of jungle paths running through Laos and Cambodia.

The South Vietnamese government, which by 1965 was led by the military regime of President Nguyen Van Thieu, did not protect its people from the war's destruction. The countryside was torn up by the bombings and the battles between guerrilla bands and government troops. Thousands of villagers died in the crossfire, and millions fled from their homes and sought shelter in Saigon and other cities. Even there, the helpless population was battered by guerrilla rocket attacks.

Throughout the conflict, the communist guerrillas retained a clear, single-minded goal: the overthrow of the Saigon government and its replacement with a regime that could be united with the Hanoi government. The Communists called the conflict a war of national liberation. Under the leadership of the brilliant North Vietnamese defense minister, Vo Nguyen Giap, the NLF fought on doggedly and launched a major assault on South Vietnamese cities and military outposts in January 1968. Known as the Tet Offensive because the fighting began during the Vietnamese New Year holiday called Tet, the NLF attack was repulsed with heavy losses for both sides.

Although defeated, the NLF offensive proved to be a crippling blow to the American war effort in Vietnam. With casualties mounting and the financial cost of the war reaching frightening levels, the American public began to demand an end to U.S. involvement in the Vietnam conflict. After reaching a peak of more than a half million men in 1968, American military strength began to decline. The bombing of North Vietnam was stopped while the U.S. government tried to negotiate an end to the war. Meanwhile, the American military prepared the Saigon government's army for the responsibility of defending South Vietnam by itself.

In June 1969, representatives from the United States and North Vietnam began holding peace negotiations in Paris. No agreement was reached at the first conferences. The NLF expanded its bases in the South, and the United States resumed its bombing of North Vietnam and helped South Vietnamese troops strike at NLF outposts in Cambodia and Laos. During 1972, NLF units captured a number of important areas in the South and threatened Saigon, but then retreated before a South Vietnamese counterattack. U.S. bombing attacks and mine-laying operations turned North Vietnam's cities into rubble and sealed off its ports.

Finally, in January 1973, the U.S. and North Vietnamese representatives at the Paris peace negotiations signed a treaty that was intended to bring about the reunification of Vietnam. The terms called for the withdrawal of all remaining U.S. troops from Vietnam, a cease-fire between NLF and South Vietnamese forces, and elections in South Vietnam that would include candidates from all political parties, including the communists. The treaty left the old border between the North and South intact until elections supervised by international mediators could decide the political future of a unified Vietnam.

The treaty did not end the fighting in Vietnam. At first, the Thieu government in Saigon was able to push back the NLF. By late 1974, however, the guerrillas had begun to rout the South Vietnamese troops. In April 1975, Saigon fell to NLF troops and the South Vietnamese army surrendered. Saigon's name was changed to Ho

Qui Nhon was one of countless South Vietnamese villages where U.S. Marines battled communist guerrillas. This boy was captured as a spy.

Chi Minh City, in honor of the former president of North Vietnam, who had died in 1969. A new government took power that included only Communist party officials. On July 2, 1976, a newly elected national assembly announced that the new name of the country was the Socialist Republic of Vietnam. Once more, Vietnam was a united country.

After the War

The war took an appalling toll on the Vietnamese people and their land. Almost 2 million Vietnamese were killed in the fighting or died from disease and starvation caused by the war's destruction. Many millions more were wounded, and nearly one-fifth of the population fled the country. The industries and agriculture of both northern and southern Vietnam had been severely damaged. Farmers plowed their fields knowing that at any moment they might set off an undetonated bomb hidden in the soil.

Rebuilding and reuniting the war-ravaged nation was a major problem for the new Vietnamese government. Supporters of the former South Vietnamese government were sent to "reeducation camps," where they were subjected to brutal punishments while being forced to renounce their old loyalties. Party officials indoctrinated the southern population with heavy doses of communist propaganda in order to change traditional beliefs and customs. However, the southerners were accustomed to a system of private ownership of property and had difficulty accepting the state-controlled economic system that was introduced by government officials from the North.

The new administration placed severe restrictions on private enterprise and exercised tight control over all industries, which worsened the country's already desperate economic conditions. About 700,000 residents of Ho Chi Minh City were forced to move to lightly populated areas of the country and become agricultural

(continued on page 57)

SCENES OF
VIETNAM

⋀ *Beyond this serene coastal lagoon, Vietnam's main highway runs toward a mountain pass called Hai Van and then north to the city of Hue, scene of fierce bombings during the war.*

◄ *The shoes of worshippers at the Cham Ponagar temple in Nha Trang show that religious belief survives despite government opposition.*

Λ *Where the Perfume River flows into the South China Sea at Hue, a farmer has tilled a garden in the rich but often-flooded delta mud. The small covered boats are called sampans; they often serve a family as home, transportation, and floating store all in one.*

⋏ *Religious and artistic objects adorn a temple altar in Hue's Thien Mu pagoda. The pottery and lacquered wood are Chinese in style; the halos of the painted figure show a Christian influence.*

⋏ *The tomb of Emperor Khai Dinh in Hue is preserved as a relic of the imperial era. Neither war nor sweeping changes in political philosophy have fully erased the traditional Vietnamese reverence for ancestors and the past.*

⋏ *Visitors to Hanoi troop into the tomb of Ho Chi Minh, leader of the Vietnamese Communist party for four decades. He governed North Vietnam until his death in 1969.*

⋀ *In recent years, the government has allowed an increasing amount of free trade, as in Hanoi's Free Market.*

⋀ *A bookstand in Hue offers government-censored newspapers along with translations of Agatha Christie's mystery novels.*

⋏ *These youngsters in Hanoi will probably benefit from recent improvements in their nation's school system, but health care, especially for infants and children, lags behind that of other countries.*

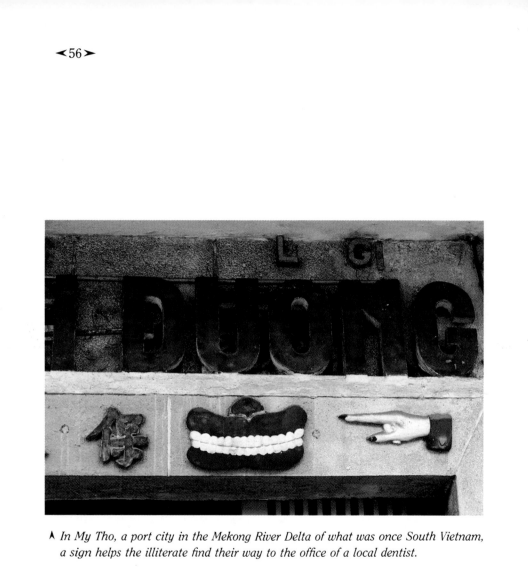

▲ *In My Tho, a port city in the Mekong River Delta of what was once South Vietnam, a sign helps the illiterate find their way to the office of a local dentist.*

(continued from page 48)

laborers in the government's special "economic zones." The former city dwellers endured constant hardships because of the shortage of food and housing in the war-ravaged economic zones.

Even after the fighting in Vietnam ended, thousands of people continued to swell the ranks of those fleeing to refugee camps in Thailand, Malaysia, and other nations in Southeast Asia. Many of these refugees were members of Vietnam's Chinese population or of other ethnic minorities that were harshly treated by the new communist regime. Thousands of them crowded into tiny boats and attempted to escape by sea. Many of these so-called "boat people" drowned or starved to death before reaching their destination, and others were robbed of all their belongings by pirates. Although some refugees were allowed to emigrate to the United States, Canada, and other countries, many more remained homeless.

In the late 1970s, the growing tensions between Vietnam and its neighbors flared into open warfare. In 1978, the Vietnamese became embroiled in a dispute with the brutal regime of the Cambodian dictator Pol Pot, which was allied with China. Vietnam, which continued to be heavily supported by the Soviet Union, invaded Cambodia in 1978, quickly occupied most of the country, and set up a government under the Cambodian leader Heng Samrin. Angered by Vietnam's treatment of its Chinese population and its invasion of Cambodia, China attacked Vietnam in early 1979. The two countries fought a brief border war before tensions eased.

Because of the controversy surrounding Vietnam's invasion of Cambodia, the Hanoi government's attempts to improve its international relations met with little success in the early 1980s. The United States and some other countries imposed trade sanctions on Vietnam after the invasion of Cambodia. The high cost of maintaining troops in Cambodia hindered economic growth, diverting the country's resources into military expenditures. Vietnam's standard of living during this period remained among the lowest in the world.

Vietnam's occupation of neighboring Cambodia turned thousands of Cambodians into refugees. These people are fleeing to Thailand.

But in 1986, three members of the country's former hard-line regime resigned, paving the way for a more moderate administration. The new leaders began to loosen government control over private enterprise. Also in the 1980s, the United States and Vietnam developed an active relationship covering a range of humanitarian issues, particularly the U.S. desire to account for American military people missing since the war. The countries agreed to handle these issues as a separate, humanitarian agenda, without reference to political differences.

This relationship was strengthened in 1992 when sweeping changes to Vietnam's constitution were approved. The new constitution marked the beginning of a major restructuring of the government. However, it also reaffirmed the continued role of the Communist party as the leading force in the state.

In 1993, as progress was made in recovering the remains of American servicemen, the United States dropped its objection to lending to Vietnam. In 1994, the U.S. trade embargo was lifted; in 1995, the two countries announced the restoration of diplomatic relations; and in 1997, the first U.S. ambassador since the Vietnam War arrived in Hanoi.

Today, Vietnam is enjoying remarkable industrial and economic growth, largely because of a surge in foreign investment and the loosening of government restrictions on free trade within the country. A number of economic problems persist. For example, the unemployment rate remains high, and the financial and legal structures required to maintain economic growth are not yet strong. But the current situation has stirred hopes that a stormy and divisive era in Vietnamese history has finally ended.

Most Vietnamese have broad faces, high cheekbones, dark eyes, and straight black hair. In spite of these common features, there is great ethnic diversity in the country.

People
and Culture

Vietnamese culture is the product of the blending of many different peoples who have merged to form a fascinatingly complex society. Through the centuries, the Vietnamese have developed a society that has emphasized the traditional values of the agricultural way of life and devotion to the family and village. In the face of the increasing influence of urban life and the international marketplace on Vietnamese society, customs and beliefs have inevitably begun to change. But the cultural bonds that have held the Vietnamese together through long periods of foreign occupation remain the foundation of modern Vietnam.

About 85 percent of Vietnam's 74 million people are members of the dominant national racial group, ethnic Vietnamese. The rest of the population belongs to the Khmer, Jarai, Chinese-Vietnamese, or another of the country's 60 minority groups, each of which has its own distinct customs. Because most of the people live near the eastern coastal areas, traditional Vietnamese culture reflects the way of life of the sedentary lowland farmers rather than the nomadic highland tribes.

The Vietnamese share many common physical features. Most Vietnamese have broad faces, high cheekbones, dark eyes, straight black hair, and light to medium brown skin. Like most of the people of East Asia, the Vietnamese have epicanthic folds on their eyelids, which makes their eyes appear long and slanted. Men average about 5 feet 2 inches (1.56 meters) in height and weigh about 120 pounds (54 kilograms). Most Vietnamese women are slightly taller and lighter than the men.

The Vietnamese tend to think that northerners and southerners have regional characteristics. In general, northerners are viewed as being more conservative, more bound to their communities, and more enterprising than the people of the warmer and less densely populated South, who are considered more easy-going and more open to foreign influences. The regional differences are not always obvious to foreigners, but they have played a part in the conflicts and rivalries that have divided Vietnam into warring sections.

Vietnam's present government has been struggling to form a unified nation and to lessen the differences between northerners and southerners. To bind the people together under one system of beliefs, the government has been working to replace traditional Confucianist and Buddhist teachings with communist doctrines and to transfer the Vietnamese loyalty from their families to the national state. The Vietnamese are extremely proud of their ancient heritage, however, and so far they have resisted any massive changes in their society.

Minority Groups

Vietnam's minority groups have made major contributions to the development of Vietnamese culture. Some groups, such as the Khmer and Cham, are descendants of the people who once ruled over parts of what are now Vietnam. Others, such as the Thai and Man, are descended from nomadic tribes that migrated into the northern and western highland regions. Finally, there are the Chinese-Vietnamese, who have long composed an important part of the country's urban economy.

The Chinese-Vietnamese are the largest of the country's minority ethnic groups, numbering about 1 million and living mainly in the cities of the South. In the past, the Chinese-Vietnamese used their overseas connections and their skill in business matters to establish themselves as Vietnam's most powerful bankers, lenders, and traders. Living together in special urban areas, such as the Cholon district in Saigon, they avoided being absorbed into mainstream Vietnamese society. However, the Chinese and Vietnamese have shared similar cultures and have celebrated many of the same festivals and religious rites.

In recent times, the governments of both South Vietnam and the Socialist Republic of Vietnam made strong attempts to assimilate the ethnic Chinese into the larger society. After the country was unified in 1975, the Communist government stripped the Chinese-Vietnamese of their businesses and much of their private property. Hundreds of thousands of Chinese-Vietnamese fled over the northern border to China or joined the "boat people" exodus by sea. The loss of so many energetic and educated people was a tragic blow to Vietnam's culture and economy. Since the late 1980s, however, the persecution has eased.

The Vietnamese have had greater success at absorbing some of the other ethnic groups. Only about 20,000 descendants of the people who ruled the kingdom of Champa still exist. Most of the Chams, who live mainly in central Vietnam, are Muslims. Ruins of their once grand temples and citadels can still be seen in the countryside.

Vietnam's 350,000 Khmer are concentrated in the Mekong Delta region. Although the Khmer have been well integrated into Vietnamese society, their close relationship to the people of Cambodia has been a frequent source of trouble between the Cambodian and Vietnamese governments. Most Khmer are rice farmers.

The tribes that occupy the highland regions have historically maintained a distinct way of life and have had little contact with the rest of Vietnam. Most of them are the descendants either of Indonesian peoples who settled Vietnam in early times or of tribes that originated in southern China. Although the highland tribes are sometimes grouped together under the name Montagnard, they are also known by the names of individual groups, such as the Man, Jarai, Thai, and Muong.

The highland tribes hunt, fish, and practice a seminomadic form of agriculture, in which they clear a plot of land and farm it until the soil has been exhausted. They commonly live in villages of bamboo huts mounted on stilts. Many of the tribes practice forms of nature worship and magic rituals, in which sorcerers make offerings to animal spirits to win good luck.

Recently, the Vietnamese government has been making greater efforts to bring the hill peoples into closer contact with the main Vietnamese society. However, they remain the most isolated and least educated segment of Vietnam's population.

Languages and Dialects

Vietnamese is the official language of Vietnam, although many other languages and dialects are used by the country's different ethnic groups. Originally derived from the speech of the tribes that settled in the Red River region, Vietnamese includes elements of other languages, including Chinese and French. Like many other Asian languages, Vietnamese uses tones and pitches, which gives the speech a somewhat musical quality. The meaning of a word depends on which of the language's six tones is used when pronouncing it. The word *ma*, for instance, may mean cheek, horse, ghost, coffin, bush, or but. Codes of etiquette and personal behavior are also reflected in the language. There are 15 ways of expressing the word "I," depending on who is being addressed.

The language that has had the strongest influence on Vietnamese is Chinese. During the 1,000-year period in which China ruled over Vietnam, the Chinese language and script was used by administrators and poets. Later, the Vietnamese rulers decreed that Vietnamese was the official language. For greater ease in writing in their own language, Vietnamese scholars developed a script called *chu nom*, which was a simplified form of Chinese characters.

At the beginning of the 17th century, Portuguese and French missionaries invented *quoc ngu*, which is a form of the Vietnamese language using Latin letters like those used in English. The language's tones were indicated by a complex system of marks. The new script was not immediately accepted by Vietnamese intellectuals, who resented the presence of Europeans in their country. By the beginning of the 20th century, however, quoc ngu had largely replaced chu nom as the official form of written Vietnamese and was being taught in public schools along with French. Quoc ngu, now in general use, served as the device through which Western ideas and scientific learning were introduced into Vietnamese society.

Religion

Many different religions have been important in shaping the beliefs and customs of the Vietnamese. The nature worship practiced by the earliest Vietnamese has been combined with elements of the three traditional faiths—Confucianism, Buddhism, and Taoism—to create a great variety of different religious creeds. The Vietnamese have also included the teachings of Christianity and Western philosophies in their spiritual beliefs.

Organized religion has not fared well under Communist rule. After coming to power, the Communist party leaders waged a determined campaign to replace traditional religious teachings with their own revolutionary doctrines. They forced the closing of temples and churches throughout the country. But by the late 1980s, in line with the general liberalization taking place, the government's attitude toward religion softened to some degree, and formal worship has been revived.

Cao Dai worshipers are shown at prayer in their chief temple. The Cao Dai sect is one of several religions that originated during the 20th century.

Throughout the ages, Confucianism has been the guiding force behind the daily behavior and social relations of the Vietnamese. More a way of life than a religion, Confucianism is a code of ethics developed by the 6th-century B.C. Chinese scholar Confucius. In accordance with Confucianist beliefs about the importance of honoring one's parents and ancestors, Vietnamese families have traditionally maintained special places in their homes for honoring their deceased relatives with sacred rituals. Confucianism places a premium on education and learning, and its system of beliefs has long been taught in Vietnamese schools. Scholars and public officials have used Confucianist codes as guides to their thoughts and in the conduct of state affairs.

Whereas Confucianism teaches that a person must faithfully perform certain rituals and fulfill his social responsibilities in order to ensure peace and harmony in his world, Buddhism is concerned with helping a person achieve a spiritual purity that is supposed to free him from the human suffering and evil that exist in the material world. Many Buddhist sects have established themselves in Vietnam, and they have often been at the forefront of movements calling for social and political changes. Buddhist monasteries and temples are scattered throughout the country, and some groups operate schools and hospitals staffed by shaven-headed monks and nuns in their orange, yellow, or gray robes.

Taoism has exerted much less influence on Vietnamese religion than either Confucianism or Buddhism, but its priests are viewed as powerful magicians and they play an important role in village rituals. Stating that the world is controlled by a host of battling gods, spirits, and demons, Taoist philosophy teaches that individuals should strive to maintain an inner calm in the face of natural calamities.

Christianity has survived numerous periods of official persecution in Vietnam. In the past, missions established by Roman Catholic and Protestant clergymen provided medical and educational services for Vietnam's poor and won millions of converts. Vietnamese Catholics were politically powerful in the South, and during the 1960s they had frequent clashes with Buddhist groups. After the Communists took control, many churches and missions were closed, sparking a huge exodus of Catholics from the country. Although not as active as in the past, many Christian denominations have reached agreements with the government and have been allowed to continue their operations.

Vietnam has been the birthplace of many religious sects that have been either outgrowths of one of the major religions or combinations of many different faiths. Two that gained significant followings during the 20th century are the Hoa Hao and Cao Dai sects.

The Hoa Hao is a militant Buddhist reform movement that fought against both the French and the Vietminh after World War II, but its influence has dwindled since the 1950s. The Cao Dai sect, on the other hand, still maintains a strong following. Cao Dai is a mystical religion that blends the teachings of various Eastern and Western faiths and philosophies. Its adherents believe that their god speaks to them through the spirits of great figures of the past, which are contacted during group seances.

Customs

The Vietnamese are a reserved, self-disciplined people who frown upon loud public displays or arguments. Common Western gestures of intimacy such as kissing or touching the face in public are taboo because the spirit that resides in a person's head may be harmed by the contact. The Vietnamese believe it is impolite to look into the eyes of a person they are addressing. When they smile, they are usually expressing politeness rather than happiness. The Western custom of greeting people by shaking hands is now acceptable for men, but women generally use the traditional nod or bow.

The Vietnamese have numerous superstitions, many of them aimed at outwitting evil spirits. They believe it is wise to place mirrors by the front door so that dragons and fiends that try to enter the house will see their images and be frightened away. Cutting fingernails or toenails at night is considered unlucky, as is leaving chopsticks in a bowl of food. Wedding gifts that consist of only one item are believed to put a jinx on a marriage; therefore, a bride and groom should always be given two bracelets rather than one.

Vietnamese names are given in the reverse of the order generally followed by Westerners, with the family name coming first and the personal name last. However, because people are usually referred to by their personal names in both formal and informal usage, it is still the last name that is used in addresses. Names carry great symbolic importance for the Vietnamese, and many of them have secret names, known only to themselves and their parents. If the secret name is accidentally disclosed to enemies, a person is supposedly vulnerable to attacks by evil spirits.

The Vietnamese festival calendar includes a mixture of religious and political holidays. The Tet New Year's celebration, which usually occurs in January or early February, is the most important holiday. It is a time of feasts, firecracker displays, and gift-giving. During Tet, the Vietnamese decorate their houses with flowers and set aside time for paying debts and making peace with enemies. Another important festival is Wandering Souls' Day, which falls in mid-July. On this date, the souls of the dead are supposedly let out of hell for a night, and they can return to their home villages and receive food and clothing left for them by their relatives. People also leave special offerings in temples for friendless "wandering souls" so that they will not have to drift around aimlessly on a black cloud.

Family Life

Traditional blood ties and the sense of family unity remain strong in spite of the government's efforts to switch citizens' loyalties to the state. However, as more and more Vietnamese have left their home villages for large cities, the rules and ceremonies governing familial duties have begun to change.

The Vietnamese are raised in extended families that usually include members of three or more generations. In fact, every family considers itself to be part of a larger kinship group that reaches back through the ages. Most Vietnamese still pay at least some heed to the cult of the ancestor, which is based on the belief that a person's spirit lives on after death and is able to affect events in the world. The sacrificial offerings that families make to their ancestors are supposed to nourish the souls of the revered relatives and to help ensure that the living family members are blessed with good luck.

Funerals are often elaborate ceremonies. Mourners traditionally wear white, and food, wine, and incense are offered to the departing spirit.

The oldest male is the head of each family, and he is given the respect of all other members of the household. Parents believe that it is extremely important to have a son to carry on the family name. All family members are part of a closely knit unit that works, eats, and worships together. Women are supposed to be subservient to their husbands and parents, but many exert a strong influence over family affairs. Children are expected to be attentive to their parents and older relatives and to care for them in their old age.

The traditional age for marriage is between 16 and 18 years for women and between 19 and 21 years for men. In the past, parents and other family elders usually chose suitable partners for young people, but now it is more common for young men and women to select their partners. However, the couple still tries to gain the approval of their parents, and it is also believed necessary to get a favorable horoscope reading about the match from a local fortune teller.

Before the marriage, gifts of cakes, nuts, and teas are exchanged between the families of the bride and groom. Families often spend a great deal of their savings on banquets, parades, and firecrackers to celebrate the marriage of their children. At the end of the wedding ceremony, the bride and groom take bites out of a piece of ginger that has been rubbed in salt. This ritual is supposed to ensure that the marriage will survive even the harshest times.

The birth of a child is greeted with much festivity. Newborn children are expected to be already somewhat wise in the ways of the world, because it is believed that while in their mother's womb, they have heard and understood the conversations taking place around them. One month after the child is born, friends of the family gather for a ceremony in which offerings are made to a friendly spirit, who is supposed to protect the child. The Vietnamese have a superstition against complimenting a newborn child too loudly because they fear that jealous evil spirits will harm or kidnap the child.

Funeral ceremonies are often extravagant and expensive. Many of the rituals that are performed to help the dead enter the spirit world are elements of the cult of the ancestor. Generally, after relatives and friends have paid their respects and placed rice and coins in the mouth of the deceased, the body is wrapped in a white silk shroud and placed in a coffin. Wailing mourners carrying incense sticks, flowers, banners, and offerings of cakes and wines accompany the body to the grave site. Once the priests have spoken their prayers for the dead, the coffin is lowered into the grave, along with food and drink to sustain the person in the afterworld.

Food and Clothing

The Vietnamese diet revolves around rice, and great importance is placed on its proper preparation at meals. A pot of burned rice is sometimes believed to be an omen of future troubles. Rice is eaten with vegetables, fish, and pork, as well as a variety of nutritious and tasty sauces made from beans, hot spices, and fish. Rice wine is often served with dinners, especially in village households. Villagers dine sitting on straw mats placed on the floor, while city residents more often use tables. The food is eaten with chopsticks or spoons.

In the cities, people frequently choose *pho*, a soup made with noodles and organ meats, for their midday meals. The Vietnamese are also extremely fond of making lunches of *nuoc mam* — fish sauce — which they pour on rice balls. Children like to snack on fruits and sweet cakes.

In the early years of the Communist regime, Vietnamese who worked in the cities commonly ate in government-operated dining halls, and ration cards were used for household food supplies. In today's Vietnam, however, the city streets are peppered with street vendors, stalls, and outdoor markets. There are even bustling shopping districts in major cities, selling handicrafts such as lacquerware vases, ceramics, and clothing.

Clothing styles vary somewhat by region. In the North, both men and women commonly wear plain black trousers with white or black jackets. In the South, most people dress in traditional loose-fitting shirts with pants or shorts. In southern cities, particularly Ho Chi Minh City, young Vietnamese can be seen in the American-influenced fashion of tee-shirts and jeans. For farmers, broad, conical hats that protect the head from the sun are especially popular. Villagers usually go barefoot, but city residents

often wear sandals or wooden shoes that have rubber soles cut from old tires.

Perhaps the most uniquely Vietnamese style of dress is the *ao dai*, which is commonly worn by women in southern towns and cities. It consists of a high-necked, long-sleeved shirt that has pieces of cloth hanging down to the ankles in the front and back. Black or white satin pants are worn under the shirt, which is often made from brilliantly colored embroidered cloth.

The colors and fabrics of clothes have long played an important part in marking social position in Vietnam. In ancient times, government officials wore blue garments made of silk, while commoners wore brown or gray clothes made from coarser materials. After the Communist victory, in an effort to promote social equality, the government encouraged the wearing of simple clothes made from black, white, or gray cloth.

Art and Literature

Vietnamese artists and poets have always borrowed many literary and artistic styles and themes from the Chinese and other East Asian peoples, but from these influences they have fashioned their own distinct cultural heritage. The most common form of traditional Vietnamese sculpture is the stone panels that were carved with mythological symbols and supernatural animals and placed on the columns and walls of temples and pagodas. In the past, Vietnamese painters have taken much of their subject matter from Chinese landscape artists, who used natural settings to render human emotions. During the 20th century, many Vietnamese artists have broadened their range to include French and Western artistic styles.

The Vietnamese are skilled craftworkers and artisans, and they produce many types of handicrafts for foreign markets. Some products, such as silk embroideries, are chiefly decorative. Others, such as the intricate baskets woven by village craftspeople, are important

In a handicraft school in Hue, boys are taught the traditional art of painting on lacquered vases and statues.

parts of everyday work life. The Vietnamese are famed for their skill in making fine gold jewelry and producing lacquer-work designs on tables and wood panels. Other specialties include pottery and ceramic work, ivory and tortoise shell carving, and leather work.

Music has traditionally been associated with religious rituals or theater shows. Among the most popular entertainers today are balladeers, usually women, who sing old folk tunes or sad love songs. The singers often perform with bands. Groups that play classical Vietnamese music use a variety of guitars, gongs, trumpets, drums, and wooden percussion instruments. The one-stringed *don doc huyen* is one of the most often played instruments and is valued for its ability to produce sounds that resemble the human voice.

Theater is another form of popular entertainment in Vietnam. There are three main types of theater. In *Hat Boi*, which takes tragic or weighty moral dramatic themes for its subjects, heavily costumed actors play the parts of legendary creatures and heroic warriors who engage in a series of adventures to prove some moral point. The actors often wear beards, which they pull and stroke to convey different emotions. Feelings are also shown by gestures with the fingers and arms. The Vietnamese also have comic theater, *Hat Cheo*, and a more modern type of traveling theater, *Cai Luong*, that presents tragic and comic plays that are highlighted with spectacular stages, costumes, and music.

Poetry has always occupied the highest position in Vietnamese literature. Borrowing from Chinese literary styles, Vietnamese poets developed an impressive variety of verse forms and symbols to discuss such subjects as traditional Confucianist philosophy, the struggle for national independence, and the harmony or conflict that exists between humans and nature. One classic poem describes the troubled sleep of a political exile dreaming about his home. It was written by the renowned 15th-century poet Nguyen Trai, who was the chief counsel of Le Loi, the heroic king who expelled the Chinese imperial forces from Vietnam.

Inside the silent, gloomy room,
all night I listen to the rain.
Its dirge disturbs an exile's pillow.
It drips and drops as wane late hours.
It drums on windows and bamboos.
With tolling bells, it enters dreams.
I've hummed a song and stayed awake.
Sleep comes by bits and shreds till dawn.

The long, sad epic *Kim Van Kieu* (*Tale of Kieu*) has become known as the Vietnamese national poem. Written in the late 18th century by the scholar Nguyen Du, the poem describes the adventures of a young woman who undergoes a series of marriages and extreme hardships before she is reunited with her first love. To many Vietnamese, the troubles and ultimate triumph of the heroine Kieu

This portrait of an actor in traditional clothing was made in 1887. Vietnamese theater includes serious dramas and popular comedies.

A photograph from 1923 shows a band of Vietnamese musicians. The round metal drums are hung by cords over the musicians' shoulders and struck with their fists.

symbolize the past misfortunes of their own war-torn and divided country.

In recent times, prose works have gained greater prominence, and some have been translated into English. Bao Ninh's *The Sorrow of War* (1991) recounts the author's wartime experiences and the postwar demoralization he witnessed. Duong Thu Huong, who spent some time in prison for her writings, has portrayed the war and the problems of the Communist system in novels like *Paradise of the Blind* (1988) and *Novel Without a Name* (1995).

Much new building, as well as rebuilding of old or damaged structures is going on in major cities. Nonetheless, the housing shortage is severe.

Cities and Villages

The Vietnamese way of life changed little before the establishment of French rule in the mid-1800s. Since then, Vietnam's cities have become economic centers and have attracted large numbers of people from rural areas. As the Vietnamese have moved to urban areas in search of greater work opportunities, the cities have been strained to meet the needs of their swelling populations.

Houses and public buildings in Vietnam's cities were heavily damaged during the war years. Because of extreme overcrowding in metropolitan areas and the lack of funds available for constructing modern buildings, housing conditions have been slow to improve. In the warm climate of the South, most families live in homes with walls and roofs made of palm leaves or straw. In the cooler northern regions, many people build simple wood or bamboo houses with tiled roofs. A smaller number of houses, mainly those of upper-level bureaucrats and businessman, are constructed of brick or stone.

Another reminder of the war years that continues to trouble the Vietnamese is the large number of Amerasians (the children of Vietnamese mothers and American fathers) who live in Ho Chi Minh City. Most Amerasians have never been completely accepted in Vietnamese society, and many have had to turn to begging to stay alive.

Nevertheless, the nation's remarkable economic progress since the late 1980s offers hope for the cities. In many cities, Vietnamese are currently experiencing a slow but steady increase in their quality of life. Today, about 90 percent of all families in Ho Chi Minh City own at least one motorbike. More important, they are also more likely than they were 20 years ago to have basic amenities like running water, electricity, and toilets.

Vietnam has three cities with populations of more than 1 million. The sprawling southern metropolis of Ho Chi Minh City has about 4 million residents and is larger than the northern cities of Hanoi and Haiphong. The center of Ho Chi Minh City extends southwestward from the west bank of the Saigon River and merges with the Cholon district, the Chinese section. With its large number of cafes, the city was once thought to have an appearance and cultural atmosphere reminiscent of Paris. Many buildings are plastered with a light stucco material that was popular during the French colonial era, but many older structures have decayed in recent times.

Ho Chi Minh City is the entertainment capital of Vietnam, although the city is much more sedate than it was during the years of the American presence in the country. The police are on the streets in full force at night to ensure that people remain well-behaved, but the city still has a much livelier cultural atmosphere than Hanoi. More foreign goods, such as canned food, soap, and television sets are available on the black market in Ho Chi Minh City than in the capital city.

Along with entertainment and the black market, Ho Chi Minh City provides southern Vietnam's main center of manufacturing and distribution of goods. The city's factories make textiles, bicycles, and handicrafts. Shipyards and leather tanneries are also important. In the commercial center of the city, new high-rise hotels and offices have sprouted. Because the citizens rarely used the city's official Communist name anyway, this business district is now generally called Saigon, the old name for the entire urban area.

Hanoi is the seat of the national government and the second-largest city in Vietnam. Under French rule, Hanoi won a reputation for being one of the most attractive cities in Asia, and the charm of its broad tree-lined boulevards and shady parks is still evident. American bombing raids in the 1960s and 1970s destroyed much of the city, but most of it has since been rebuilt. The one-man bomb shelters that were dug into the pavement on the edges of streets during the war years have been filled in. Monuments to the communist workers' state now line the streets and plazas.

Compared to Ho Chi Minh City, Hanoi is a much smaller, quieter, cleaner place, still reflecting the intellectual austerity of the Communist leaders who fought for decades for a united, socialist Vietnam. But with the new economy stressing foreign investment and tourism, the city is bubbling with plans for office towers, large new apartment buildings, and hotels. Motorcycles are beginning to compete with motorbikes and bicycles for dominance on the streets. Some observers feel that if Hanoi's expansion is not carefully controlled, the environment and liveability of the city may be seriously damaged.

A principal attraction of Hanoi is Petit Lac, a lake in the center of the city. On a small island in the lake stands the Turtle Pagoda, which marks the spot where legends say a turtle rose from the water bearing a sword with which an ancient Vietnamese hero drove out Chinese invaders. Another popular attraction, near the lake, is the mausoleum that contains the body of Ho Chi Minh, the founder of the Vietnamese Communist party.

Haiphong, which is about 55 miles to the east of Hanoi, is a major industrial center and seaport. Its factories produce cement, china, glass, phosphates, and textiles. Products shipped to Haiphong are carried by railroad to Hanoi. During the war years, Haiphong became North Vietnam's major point of entry for military supplies, and the city was heavily bombed by American planes. The city's battle scars have not healed as quickly as those of Hanoi.

In the central portion of Vietnam lie the smaller but well-known cities of Hue and Da Nang. Large portions of Hue were destroyed in the Vietnam War, but the city of some 350,000 people remains a cultural and religious hub, featuring important museums and places of worship. As the former capital during the long-reigning Nguyen dynasty, it also boasts the ruins of the old imperial palace. Da Nang, about 70 miles to the south of Hue, is the country's third largest city, with a population of around 800,000. It became famous during the Vietnam War in part because of nearby "China Beach," a rest-and-recreation site for U.S. military personnel. Currently Da Nang's major role is as a port city, though its large potential for tourism remains to be tapped.

Although the urban population has swelled in recent times, 80 percent of the Vietnamese still live in farming or fishing villages. Their traditional way of life has changed far less than that of city residents. In the past, the Communist party forced many farmers to leave their home villages and work on large state-operated communes. This policy angered the farmers and was partially responsible for a series of disastrous harvests. More recently, the government has relaxed its tight control over agriculture, allowing farmers to work their own land and sell surplus produce for a profit. Some

The main streets of many towns and villages are rivers.

industrious farmers have been able to earn as much as five times the salary of an urban office worker with their private sales.

The crops grown by today's Vietnamese farmers are often exported for the world market, but agricultural methods remain little different from those used many centuries ago. Plowing is still commonly done with a team of water buffaloes, and irrigation systems are often quite primitive.

Vietnamese dignitaries (who include the Communist party chief and the prime minister) gather in Ho Chi Minh City to commemorate the anniversary of the fall of Saigon.

Government and Social Services

The Communist party is the only political party in the Socialist Republic of Vietnam. This one party, founded in the 1930s by Ho Chi Minh, has ruled a unified Vietnam since 1975. A new constitution approved in 1992 reinforced the party's authority by stating that the Vietnamese Communist party will continue to be the only legitimate political organization in the country. Although the party today numbers about 2.1 million members, many political experts question how long it can maintain its control during an era of rapid economic reform.

Until the mid-1980s, the Vietnamese government was controlled by a group of the old-guard, conservative leaders who had helped to form the Vietminh resistance group 40 years before. The three long-time Communist leaders — President Truong Chinh, Prime Minister Pham Van Dong, and powerful Politburo member Le Duc Tho — finally resigned in 1986 after a majority of high party officials agreed that the regime's rigid policies had severely damaged the nation's economy.

Nevertheless, the Communist party's Politburo, which has fewer than 20 members, remains the most powerful political force in

Vietnam. Members of the Politburo include the party's general secretary, the president, and the prime minister. The Politburo is chosen by the party's Central Committee, which has more than 100 members. Large-scale party congresses, at which major policy changes are discussed and ratified, are held every few years.

The president is the head of state and also the commander of the armed forces. The prime minister heads a cabinet whose members include three deputy prime ministers and directors of the nation's various ministries and commissions.

Vietnam's legislative authority is the National Assembly, which has roughly 500 deputies who are elected for five-year terms. During its twice-yearly meetings, the National Assembly gathers to approve the Politburo's decisions and the Communist party's proposals for legislation. The 1992 constitutional revision did give the Assembly greater independence and more authority over defense and finance than it had held before. Also as a result of that constitutional change, Assembly members need not belong to the Communist party.

Corruption, unfortunately, is a major problem within the government, and it is difficult to challenge because genuine dissent is not permitted. The government continues to prohibit an independent press. In 1993, for example — even after the economic liberalization had begun — a new law barred the publication of works deemed hostile to socialism in Vietnam.

On a regional level, Vietnam is divided into 50 provinces and three independent municipalities. The provinces are further divided into cities, towns, and villages. All of these areas, whether large provinces or small villages, are administered by elected bodies known as People's Councils, which choose committees to take care of daily business. These local agencies have minimal authority, but they are charged with distributing resources, developing economic plans, and ensuring public order. Their function is basically administrative rather than legislative.

These students of agronomy, or agricultural science, will be called upon to help their country increase its food production through better farming.

Education and Health Care

After the division of the country in 1954, both North Vietnam and South Vietnam made special efforts to expand their educational systems. However, more than 3,000 schools were destroyed during the war and little money could be spared for education. Since 1975, the government has been trying to rebuild the school system, and the situation has improved dramatically.

Education throughout the country is free, and students are required to finish 12 years of schooling. Class instruction includes much discussion of Communist doctrines, but the sciences receive far less attention. There are about 8 million students in elementary-level education and 4 million at the secondary level. Classrooms tend to be extremely crowded because there is a dire shortage of trained teachers.

The country has about 90 universities and colleges and 287 vocational schools where specialized skills are taught. Between 1981

These children can receive 12 years of free schooling, but many schools were destroyed during the war, and classes today are crowded.

and 1986 alone, 150,000 students graduated from universities in Vietnam, and 178,000 received vocational training. The government claims nearly to have eliminated illiteracy, and the official literacy rate is placed at 94 percent, meaning that 94 percent of adults can read and write.

Families with well-placed connections in the government can sometimes arrange for their children to study abroad. These privileged students can expect to hold influential positions in the government upon their return to their native country. Until recently, however, opportunities for students with science or business degrees have been limited by the slow progress of the nation's industry and agriculture.

Vietnam's social welfare system attempts to provide health services to those in villages and rural areas, as well in the cities. But health care in much of the country is fairly rudimentary. Part of the health care problem is caused by a tremendous shortage of professional health care workers, as well as a shortage of facilities to provide medical services. The country has only one doctor per 2,500 people and just one hospital bed for every 366 people.

The Ministry of Health has been waging an intensive campaign to eliminate such potentially deadly diseases as typhoid, tuberculosis, and diphtheria, all of which have been virtually eliminated in the Western world through immunization. Serious food shortages in recent years have created a large malnutrition problem in urban areas. In the 1980s and 1990s, the spread of the HIV virus and AIDS became a major concern. On the positive side, however, modest improvements in health care have decreased the death rate and improved the average life expectancy. In 1981, the average Vietnamese could expect to live only to age 52. Now the life expectancy is about 65 years for men and 70 years for women.

Vegetables and fruits fill the markets of a country dominated by agriculture. In recent years, droughts and floods have caused many poor harvests.

Resources
and Economy

Vietnam's economy has been beset by major problems during the period following the country's unification. During the war years, South Vietnam received large amounts of foreign aid from the United States, while North Vietnam was supported by the Soviet Union and China. Much of the aid was for military equipment that provided no economic benefits. After the end of the war, however, Vietnam was forced to reconstruct its shattered economy with little foreign aid from any country except the Soviet Union. The Vietnamese government's costly takeover of Cambodia in 1979 did not help matters, nor did its rigid economic policies. For more than a decade after reunification, the government owned and controlled almost all the factories, farms, and other businesses. The government bureaucracy, instead of stimulating economic initiative, too often tended to stifle it. Industries languished, and inflation raged. After the beginnings of economic liberalization in the late 1980s, the government courted and was able to attract more foreign investment, and since then the economic situation has improved.

Despite all the changes that have taken place, Vietnam's economy continues to be based on agriculture. Far more than half of the nation's workers are farmers, and rice is their most important crop.

Farming equipment is in short supply, however, and the harvests have often been damaged by droughts, floods, and typhoons. In 1994 alone, environmental disasters cost the Vietnamese a million tons of rice.

About 15 percent of the land in northern Vietnam and 20 percent of the land in southern Vietnam is used for farming. Most of the rest is unsuitable for growing crops. Besides rice, food products grown in Vietnam include coffee, coconuts, corn, cotton, sugarcane, sweet potatoes, and a tropical plant called cassava, from which tapioca is made. Rubber, coffee, tea, and many other crops are raised primarily for export. Peanuts, sesame, castor beans, and soybeans are grown for vegetable oil producing factories and are an important part of total agricultural production. Pigs and poultry are the two major types of livestock, but the government has had some success in increasing the number of cattle raised for beef production.

Fish and shellfish caught from inland waters and from the South China Sea are the second most important food after rice. Most of the catch, which includes large amounts of tuna, mackerel, and sardines, is sold fresh on the home market, but some is frozen or dried in processing factories and exported to other Asian countries.

After rice, fish and shellfish are the main food items.

Forestry products are another important part of Vietnam's agricultural exports. The majority of the hardwood timber is harvested from the highland regions of the North. Pine and oak are cut for building construction, and a variety of precious woods such as teak and ebony are harvested for furniture and handicrafts. Bamboo is grown throughout the country for use in domestic housing construction. Cinnamon, anise, and other spices that grow in the forests are also valuable products. Although there has been little modernization in the forestry industry, production has been slowly expanding.

Vietnam's manufacturing, construction, and mining industries developed little under the socialist system. Much of the country's industrial production continued to be performed at home or in small shops. Many of the aging factories operated at half of their capacities because they lacked power, raw materials, or spare parts. With the new capitalist-style initiatives — and the funds being offered by agencies like the International Monetary Fund, the World Bank, and the Asian Development Bank — the Vietnamese government hopes to make substantial strides in modernizing not only its industries but also the transportation system that the factories need to get their products to market. Currently the country's major industries include food processing, textiles, cement, glass, and tires. In addition, Vietnam makes large amounts of fertilizer from phosphate. Because northern Vietnam has rich deposits of coal, gold, iron, chromite, zinc, and tin, much of the heavy industry is located around Hanoi and Haiphong.

Most of Vietnam's electrical power is produced by coal-burning plants. The country's first nuclear reactor for research purposes began operating in 1984. The country is currently studying the possibility of building a nuclear power plant in the future. There are also projects under way to build more hydroelectric plants. Despite Vietnam's attempts to expand its power generation capacity, a large part of the population does not have electricity at home. Even in the

North Vietnam has rich deposits of coal; mining and exporting coal is a major source of revenue.

cities, blackouts frequently occur because of shortages of fuel and spare parts.

After years of trying to attract investors from Asian and Western countries, Vietnam welcomed a surge of foreign funding in the years following the removal of the U.S. embargo. Between 1993 and 1995, foreign investments increased 50 percent, and they have continued at high levels since then. Major investing countries include Japan, Australia, Malaysia, France, and the United States, among others.

Vietnam still imports more goods from other countries than it exports. Crude oil is the country's largest single export, accounting for about one-quarter of total exports, slightly more than manufactures. The country's other key exports include rubber, rice, coal, fish, coffee, and garments. Imports include petroleum products, machinery and equipment, steel products, raw cotton, and grain.

Despite the rapid economic growth of recent years, the Vietnamese still have a large national debt. The country must also deal with recurrent problems of inflation and unemployment. There is concern, too, that the government may not be proceeding quickly enough to establish a legal and financial infrastructure strong enough to support the economy as it continues to expand.

In the coastal regions and along the many rivers, travel by boat is the most common means of transportation.

Transportation and Communications

Historically, travel in Vietnam has been done mainly by foot and oxcart or by boats and ships in coastal regions and areas near the major rivers. Because the terrain in much of the country is either rugged or marshy, the road system has never grown very large. When the French ruled Vietnam, they built an extensive railway network, but bridges and tracks were heavily damaged during the fighting in the 1960s and 1970s. The rail system has been only partly repaired, and Vietnam continues to suffer from a shortage of spare parts for all means of transportation.

For short distances, most Vietnamese either walk or use bicycles or motorbikes. During the daytime hours, the streets of large cities often become a tangled mass of pedestrians and bicyclists. The country has 65,000 miles (105,000 kilometers) of roads, but only 10 percent of this total is paved. Few people have their own automobiles, but commercial vehicles are more common, and motorcycles are now joining motorbikes on city streets. The transportation system also includes urban and long-distance buses and over 1,600 miles (2,600 kilometers) of railway.

The country's national airline, Hang Kong Vietnam, operates a fleet of more than 30 jetliners. It has passenger service from Hanoi to nine Vietnamese cities and from Ho Chi Minh City to six other cities. The airline also flies from Vietnam to Moscow, Berlin, Prague, Paris, and Bangkok, among other cities. Airlines from more than 20 other countries also serve Vietnam.

In a country whose major cities are either on the coast or a short distance inland, water transportation is naturally of great importance. Vietnam has three main seaports: Haiphong, Da Nang, and Ho Chi Minh City. Its merchant fleet includes 112 vessels and has routes to ports in Japan, Hong Kong, Singapore, Russia, and other trading partners in Asia. Ships range from large freighters to the traditional wooden sailing vessels called sampans. The number of trawlers and small boats used in Vietnam's important fishing industry has declined in recent years because many of them were taken from the country at the time of the boat people exodus. Travel on the river branches and canals of Vietnam's delta regions is usually done on small cargo boats and barges.

In Hanoi and elsewhere, the bicycle is more important than the car or bus for getting around.

In Vietnam's highly regimented communist society, all types of public communications media are subject to government censorship. The Communist party leaders believe that the duty of the press is to promote loyalty to the nation rather than to give objective viewpoints about news events and issues. Journalists are forbidden to criticize government policies, and thus the public has a difficult time learning about the true condition of the country. However, party leaders do on occasions stir up national debates by printing newspaper articles that attack waste and corruption in government and business. In their articles, the officials sometimes encourage readers to write to the newspaper with reports about incompetent managers and unfair laws.

Vietnam has four large daily newspapers: *Nhan Dan*, *Hanoi Moi*, and *Quon Doi Nhan Dan* of Hanoi and *Saigon Giai Phong* of Ho Chi Minh City. The combined daily circulation of these newspapers and other smaller publications is about 500,000. *Nhan Dan*, the Communist party newspaper, is the official source of all news and information, and its main function is to serve as a mouthpiece for the government. Vietnamese newspapers often print poems about political subjects; these have long been a popular means of public protest.

In addition to the major newspapers, the Vietnamese can turn to a number of other media for news and entertainment. Government councils oversee the publication of magazines that cater to specific groups, such as teachers' organizations, sports clubs, youth groups, cultural societies, and trade unions. The national radio service, The Voice of Vietnam, and the central television broadcasting system, Giang Vo, present programs in a variety of languages, including French.

Radios and televisions, which were relatively scarce in Vietnamese homes before the 1960s, have become more common in recent times. By the mid-1990s there was a radio set for every 10 people

Newspapers posted on a gate find an eager audience. The papers are state-censored.

and a television for every 29. Telephones remained relatively scarce —
one for every 270 people — but the government hoped to multiply that
figure eightfold by the turn of the century. Vietnam has already digi-
tized 100 percent of its provincial switchboards, and fiber-optic and
microwave systems have been extended to all regions of the country.

Traders in Ho Chi Minh City peddle their wares on a Saturday morning. In recent years, the government has opened the door to individual commerce.

Rebuilding
the Republic

After decades of war, there is now peace in Vietnam. The Land of Two Rice Baskets is beginning to produce enough food to feed its people, and the country's industries are coming alive after many years of stagnation. Overcrowding is being eased through new public housing. Factories and the transportation system are being modernized. The government is attempting to improve agricultural techniques and expand the country's ranks of trained doctors, teachers, and business managers. Today, Vietnam is poised to become an even stronger force in Southeast Asia, one whose economic clout can match its military dominance.

At last, Vietnam is sharing in the rapid economic development taking place in many of the East Asian countries nearby. The nation's current government officials, recognizing that this is a pivotal time for Vietnam, are committed to advancing its economic health and strengthening ties with its trading partners. Vietnam's present leaders are more pragmatic than the conservative regime that governed through the mid-1980s, and they have instituted a number of economic and legislative changes that have revamped the country's fiscal health. Real political change, however, remains on the horizon.

The Vietnamese are proud, resourceful people who have endured many periods of hardship during their history. They have been willing to make many sacrifices in their quest for a strong, independent nation. Although resentful of foreign domination, the Vietnamese have been ready to learn from the ideas and experiences of other peoples. Thus, there is good reason to believe they will meet their new challenges in the years ahead.

Still, it is impossible to predict where these signs of hope will lead for the Vietnamese. The scars of their past wars and deep internal divisions are only beginning to heal. Old bombs and mines are still being dug up in rice fields, and much of the populace remains in

These women with swords are among the thousands of Vietnamese who perform ritual exercises every morning. The state encourages daily exercise.

overwhelming poverty. Though the process of national reconstruction will not be easy, perhaps the resilient spirit of the Vietnamese will carry them through the difficulties to come.

◄ G L O S S A R Y ►

Ao dai   The traditional costume of women in many areas of southern Vietnam. It features pants that are worn under a long shirt whose front and back panels hang down to the ankles.

Boat people   Refugees from southern Vietnam who fled their country in small boats after the Communist victory in 1975. Many of the boat people were members of Vietnamese minority groups.

Cai Luong   A modern form of Vietnamese theater presenting realistic stories about the human condition.

Chu nom   A transcription of Vietnamese words into simplified Chinese characters that was first used during the 13th century.

Collectivism   The system in which the government controls the production and distribution of goods and services.

Cult of the ancestor   The honoring of the spirits of dead ancestors in the belief that this will bring good luck to their living relatives.

Dong   Vietnamese unit of currency.

Guerrilla   A member of a mobile, lightly armed military force that uses quick raids from hidden bases to harass a stronger opponent.

Hat Boi   Classical form of dramatic theater that features stories and themes from Vietnamese folklore.

Hat Cheo   A simplified form of Hat Boi theater that includes some comedy.

Monsoons	Prevailing winds that blow from the southwest for half the year and from the northeast during the other months. Vietnam receives much of its rainfall during the summer monsoon months, from May to October.
Nuoc mam	A popular fermented fish sauce, very salty, which is used as a condiment with a variety of foods.
Pho	A popular soup that includes noodles and organ meats.
Politburo	Powerful ruling body of the Communist party that guides national policy.
Quoc ngu	The rendering of the Vietnamese language using Latin letters and a complicated system of signs indicating tone.
Tet	The Vietnamese New Year's celebration, which usually falls in late January or early February.
Viet Cong	Communist guerrilla forces that fought against the government of South Vietnam from the mid-1950s until 1975. The Viet Cong were supported by North Vietnam and operated from bases in densely forested areas of South Vietnam.
Vietminh	Communist league headed by Ho Chi Minh that took control of northern Vietnam in 1945. The Vietminh defeated the French at Dien Bien Phu in 1954 after more than seven years of fighting.

◄ INDEX ►

PICTURE CREDITS

AP/Wide World Photos: pp. 2, 20, 24–25, 26–27, 66, 74, 84, 92, 96; The Bettmann Archive: pp. 30, 34; Culver Pictures: pp. 32, 76; Reuters/Bettmann Newsphotos: pp. 58, 60; Taurus Photos: pp. 16, 49, 50, 51, 52 (above, below), 53, 54 (above, below), 55, 56, 78, 82, 88, 90, 98; United Nations: pp. 14, 87, 94; UPI/Bettmann Newsphotos: pp. 22–23, 40, 43, 47, 70, 77, 100, 102, 104